Monkey Shadows

Also by Sujata Bhatt
from Carcanet

Brunizem

Monkey Shadows

SUJATA BHATT

CARCANET

First published in 1991 by
Carcanet Press Limited
208-212 Corn Exchange Buildings
Manchester
M4 3BQ

British Library Cataloguing in Publication Data
Bhatt, Sujata 1956-
  Monkey shadows.
  1. India. English poetry
  I. Title
  821

  ISBN 0 85635 935 1

The publisher acknowledges financial assistance
from the Arts Council of Great Britain

Set in 11pt Palatino by Bryan Williamson, Darwen
Printed and bound in England by SRP Ltd, Exeter

for Michael Augustin
and Jenny Mira Augustin –

veritable macacos

Acknowledgements

Thanks are due to the editors of the following publications in which some of these poems, sometimes in different versions, first appeared: *PN Review, The North, Poetry Review* (U.K.); *Calyx* (U.S.A.); *Stint, die horen* (Germany)

Thanks are also due to Radio Bremen for broadcasting some of these poems, and to Jürgen Dierking for translating many of the poems into German.

Some of these poems have appeared in the following anthologies:
Poetry International Festival Anthology,
Rotterdam, The Netherlands, 1990;
Grandchildren of Albion, New Departures, U.K., 1991.

I should like to thank all of my daughter's grandparents for their many hours of patient baby-sitting, enabling me to complete this book. Special thanks are also due to Eleanor Wilner, whose careful reading and critical comments improved many poems. I am immensely grateful to the photographer Samir Pathak for his time and effort spent observing and photographing the monkeys at Mt Abu, Gujarat, after I merely inquired about the possibility of obtaining a monkey photo for the cover of this book. Yes, they are langurs!

Contents

III: *Until Our Bones Prevent Us from Going Further*

I

The Way
to Maninagar

The Langur Coloured Night

It was a cry
        to awaken the moon.

A sound to make the moon shout back.

It was the truth
        from a young langur.

It was a cry
        shining with moonlight,
a cry resounding against
white stone verandahs.

It was the langur
mirrored in that moon in the pond –
and the moon's face doubled
in the eyes of the langur.

It was the langur poised
                grim-faced
                stiff-haired
      between leaps.

It was a cry to breathe life
into the moon, the stones…

It was the langur
        just frozen, silver-jewelled with the moon.

It was the langur
        on his way to a tree.

It was a cry
        meant for no one
        but the moon – dear friend
of the langur who reveals the hiding places
of dogs, cats and even snakes.

It was the langur
        doing whatever he wanted to do

now that everyone is asleep.

The Stare

There is that moment
when the young human child
stares
at the young monkey child
who stares back –

Innocence facing
innocence in a space
where the young monkey child
is not in captivity.

There is purity
    clarity
there is a transparence
    in this stare
which lasts a long time...

eyes of water
        eyes of sky
the soul can still fall through
because the monkey
has yet to learn fear
and the human
has yet to learn fear –
        let alone arrogance.

Witnessing it all
one can count eyelashes
one can count the snails
in the grass
        while waiting
for eyes to blink
waiting to see who
will look away first.

Still the monkey looks
at the human not in the same way
he would look at leaves
or at his own siblings.

And the human looks
at the monkey knowing
this is some totally other being.

And yet, there is such good will
such curiosity brightening
                    their faces.

I would like to slip inside
that stare, to know
what the human child thinks
what the monkey child thinks
at that very moment.

Remember, the human child
is at that age
when he begins to use words
with power
but without the distance
of alphabets, of abstractions.

Mention bread
and he wants
a slice, buttered and with honey –
immediately.

Mention the cat
and he runs over
to awaken her.

The word
is the thing itself.

Language is simply
a necessary music
suddenly connected
            to the child's own heartbeat.

While the young monkey child
grows at a different rate,
looks at a tree, a bush,
at the human child
            and thinks...
Who knows what?

What remains burning
is that moment
of staring:
the two newly formed heads
balanced on fragile necks
tilting towards each other,
the monkey face
            and the human face
absorbing each other
with intense gentleness....

Maninagar Days

They are always there
just as pigeons or flies
can be *always there*
and the children have to fight them off,
especially during those hot May afternoons
when they dare to jump down from the trees
into the cool shaded spots, the corners between
the canna flower beds
still moist from the mornings watering.

Monkeys in the garden –
I'm talking about rhesus monkeys
the colour of dirt roads and khaki
                    and sometimes even of honey.
Rhesus monkeys that travel in small groups,
extended families; constantly feuding brothers, sisters,
uncles, aunts, cousins screaming through
the trees – while the grandmother sits farther away
sadly, holding on to the sleepy newborn.
Somehow they manage to make peace
before every meal.

Now and then a solitary langur:
the Hanuman-monkey, crossing the terrace
with the importance of someone going to the airport.
A lanky dancer's steps
with black hands, black feet
sharp as black leather gloves and black leather shoes
against the soft grey body.
Sharp
and yet delicate
as if they were brush-stroked in
with a Japanese flourish.
And black-faced too,
with thick tufts of silver grey eyebrows,

a bushy chin. So aloof
he couldn't be bothered
with anyone.

Some people live with rhesus monkeys
and langurs in their gardens.
To these children
the monkeys are as normal and common as dogs.
And yet, the monkeys remain magical.

The children feel closer
to the monkeys, although they never
really play together, although the monkeys
probably hate the children:
those three children, two girls and a boy
who are all a bit afraid
of the full-grown-to-their-prime males
that stretch themselves and stretch themselves
to the height of wisdom and fatherly wit.

The monkeys are not at all cuddly like toys.
No.
They are lean twirls, strong tails, fast shadows
abrupt with yellow teeth.
The monkeys are not so innocent
the elders warn,
not so content with their daily routine
for they are turning
into urban thieves, imitating
and even outdoing the crows:

One day a tall monkey leaped down on the clothesline
and stole a blinding white shirt.
Another day, a very muscular monkey
bounded out of the neighbour's house
with a huge rock of golden *gur*, solid raw sugar.
The boy was impressed. His mother
would have difficulty carrying such a load.

Still, the children treat the monkeys
as if they were children newly arrived from a foreign
country, unable to speak the language yet.

And the children's grandmother comes out
to the front door from time to time.
Just awakened from her afternoon nap, now
she readjusts her thin white sari
and squints against the sun
watching over them all –
And the faint May breeze that struggles
through the monkey crowded branches
is Hanuman's breath.
How could you know it, how could you miss it
unless you had lived
in such a garden.

Monkeys in the garden.
They are always there,
usually in the gulmuhore trees
chewing on the sour rubbery leaves
and the even more delicious bright
scarlet-orange flowers: petals
sparkling as sliced blood oranges,
water-plump green stems...

The monkeys have become everything
to the children, although
the children are not aware of it yet,
and one summer the children can't help
learning everything from them:
their noise, their shadows, their defiant stare,
the way they shake their heads,
the curve of their elbows
their weight on the trees...
In fact, without the monkeys
the trees begin to look a little barren
to the children.

Oh there are days when the monkeys refuse
to come down from the gulmuhore trees
and that makes the children jealous
and unhappy.
Oh there are days when the monkeys
never intrude, never interfere
with the children's favourite hide-outs.
Peaceful days, one would think
with the monkeys chatter-reclining and nibbling,
dozing and basking, jabbering and
lice-picking safe above in the gulmuhore trees
while the children run about exhausting
one game after another right below.
Peaceful hours one would think.
But the children are jealous
for they too love to eat
the gulmuhore flowers and leaves.

Invariably they try
to convince the monkeys to throw some flowers down
and then, that failing,
invariably they try to persuade the monkeys
to come down into their garden
(maybe with some flowers)
and then, that failing,
they are simply angry, so angry
at the monkeys, they terrify them off
into the neighbouring gardens.

Oh with monkeys like that
the children believe in Hanuman.
In their secret wishes the children reinvent
the perfect monkey: Hanuman,
wild and fierce and loyal and gentle...

One day the boy defended his sisters
single-handedly with a stick like a sword
he chased the whole band of monkeys
not up the trees but to the back of the house:
a complete disappearance.
Then there was such silence
the girls were afraid – where
had all the birds gone? And the neighbour's dog?
A few minutes later the boy returned
running, chased by the monkeys,
and the stick like a sword was in the hand
of the angry leader...

Monkeys in the garden.
Some people have monkeys
in their dreams, monkeys in their nightmares,
monkeys crossing their shadows
long after they have stopped being children
long after they have left such a garden.

Note:

Hanuman is the son of the wind god Maruti and Anjana, a
goddess turned into a monkey by a curse. Hanuman is the
most powerful, most intelligent and most learned of the
monkeys. He is also considered to be the 'Ideal of the perfect
servant: A servant who finds full realization of manhood, of
faithfulness, of obedience. The subject whose glory is in his
own inferiority' (P. Thomas, *Epics, Myths and Legends of
India*). This ideal servant-master relationship is especially
evident in Hanuman's devotion to Ramachandra in the epic
Ramayana.

The Daily Offering

It was more animal-purple
        than plant-purple,
a long sheath of a bud
that might blossom into an octopus
instead of a lotus, the child thought
as she asked her grandmother to buy it.

The lotus was for Krishna,
a luxury for the grandmother.
The girl was tired of the daily offering
of *tulsi* and *mogra* from their garden.
For once she wanted something magnificent.

That evening the grandmother showed the child
how to wrap the bud in a wet cloth
to keep it fresh through the hot night
and to prevent it
from opening too soon.

The next morning, minutes before the *puja*
while the grandmother straightened things out
the girl rushed to the room
where the sleeping lotus lay.
Gently, she lifted it and slowly
started to peel off the damp cloth.
As she did so, turning it over
on her lap
the petals slipped off, one by one at first
a pause
and then a downpour of petals in her arms –
the heavy purple softness stunning her
into an awed sadness.

The Glassy Green and Maroon

Cinderella had glass slippers
I used to believe in because
my mother has always worn
glass bangles of a special kind –
made as I thought from similar glass.

Ma's bangles are thick maroon and dark,
they are green glints and unbreakable
                    I think
because she can wear them all day:
whether she scrubs out clothes
or dishes, the glass bangles stay on.
Afraid of ruining her gold wedding bangles
she somehow trusts the glassy green
and maroon. Every day, broom in hand
she sweeps out the dust
from the verandah, from our doorsteps,
while the glass bangles catch
the morning sun, the afternoon sun...

Then finally, when she raises her arms
to undo the scarf protecting her hair,
how the glass bangles glisten, loyal
                    year after year
above her small wrists – bands of lingering light
illuminating her
who would otherwise remain hidden
with her work.

Nowadays I can't find
such sturdy bangles – not in Ahmedabad,
not in Delhi. The glass snaps
like raw spaghetti, like dry twigs
from termite emptied trees,
like rusty barbed wire,
rusty tin shack neighbourhoods
where tin roofs creak against their crookedness
break against the slightest movement
from the wind, from a dog's tail, from a child

                      who walks out the door.
The glass snaps
the bangles break.

Ajwali Ba

for my father's mother

This is a story
that I have heard
so many times, always told
by my father during dinner
always told as a sort of preface
to some new philosophical point
he wants to make.

Perhaps it's because
I've heard this story
so often that now
I no longer hear the words
my father repeats.
Instead, the scene unfolds
in my mind, deep within my soul's eye
it flickers, jerking like an old black and white
silent film.

It's past midnight
almost 1:00 a.m. and my grandfather
is about to enter the house.
He has spent the day working as usual
with the poor, trying to help
the shunned Harijans.

He has opened the door
to his own house to find my grandmother
blocking his way.
Orthodox Brahmin Ajwali Ba
asks him first to bathe
outside with a bucket of cool water somewhere
near the orchard
before coming in.

He is too tired, he pleads.
But she insists, standing just out of his reach
so he can't pollute her with his slightest touch.
Even if his long white shirt
dusty from the roads
but more filthy to her from being touched
                              by other castes – unclean
to her especially because
of those outcastes...
even if his shirt were to brush against
her sari, it would send her fuming off
to take another bath
and then to wear fresher clothes.
Knowing all this he stands
on the threshold.

She will not change
                her rules.
'Then, I'll sleep in the garden,'
he decides as he leaves.

Now there is a pause
while Nanabhai steps
            into the darkness
                        of the garden,
and Ajwali Ba stands inside
listening to the dark house
where their children sleep
                        oblivious to everything.

A few minutes later,
let's say about ten minutes later,
she rushes out of the house,
runs across the courtyard,
leaps down the steps
leading to the mango orchard
and joins him.

This is the part I like best.
I like to think of her, still
a young woman, racing down
the steps with the same haste
I felt running down those steps at eight, at seventeen,
at twenty-six...

We'll never know *what*
made her change her mind.
Perhaps she doesn't know herself.
But I can feel her sweeping gesture
her brisk strong arms
                tearing into the air –
and crescent eyebrows that I've inherited
and her impatience to understand him...

My father's narration ends here
at the spot where they lie
                beside each other.
But the film continues playing
                in my mind:
Now they are together,
Nanabhai and Ajwali Ba.
He surely slept, exhausted
dreamless.
And she?

I see her alert, thoughtful.
Knowing she can't sleep
she doesn't even bother
to close her eyes.

I see her staring at the sky
enjoying a private game
of untangling the stars
                and counting them
into their correct constellations.

Nanabhai Bhatt in Prison

At the foot of Takhteshwar hill
there is an L-shaped house
hidden from the road
by five mango trees
planted by Nanabhai Bhatt.

Huge crows swoop over
the L-shaped terrace,
red-beaked green parrots fight over
the mango trees. Some years the monsoons
sweep away too much.
It is 1930, 1936...
It is 1942:
Nanabhai sits writing for a moment
while my grandmother
gives orders to everyone.

The next day, he lands in prison again:
thrown in without a trial
for helping Gandhiji,
for Civil Disobedience.

One semester in college
I spent hours picturing him:
a thin man with large hands,
my grandfather in the middle
of the night, in the middle of writing,
between ideas he pauses to read
from Tennyson, his favourite –

A hand that can be clasped no more –
  Behold me, for I cannot sleep,
  And like a guilty thing I creep
At earliest morning to the door.

What did he make of the Northern trees?
The 'old yew', the chestnut...
and the strange season of falling leaves
that comes every year –
Did he spend hours trying
to picture it all?

I know that
as a student in Bombay
he saved and saved
and lived on one meal a day for six months
just so he could watch
the visiting English Company
perform Shakespeare...

And I spent hours
picturing his years in prison:
Winter 1943;
it is dark in his cell.
He is sixty years old.
I see him
sitting cross-legged on the floor
and I wonder what he knew
by heart, I wonder
which lines gave him the most comfort.

That semester was endless
with a restless Baltimore March
when the tight buds on the forsythia
teased our blood.
And I, impatient to get on
with other writers
had to slow down
to study that same poem.

So much information
swallowed like vitamins
            for finals –

and yet, I paused at every turn
wondering which parts he had loved.

Kankaria Lake

Sometimes the nine-year-old boy
finds it difficult
to believe this is water.

It is more like skin;
a reptile's skin –
wrinkled and rough as a crocodile's
          and green.

Bacterial green, decomposed
green – opaque and dull.

As if the lake
were a giant crocodile
he couldn't see the ends of.

Kankaria Lake is on the way
to the Ahmedabad Zoo.
Sundays he always walks across
the bridge over the lake.

In the distance he can see
a small park bordered
          by the water – dry grass
struggles to grow against the scummy lake.
The park seems always deserted.

Sometimes a gardener
or a homeless man
or a wandering storyteller
would fall asleep on the grass
                too close to the lake –
and soon enough the newspapers
would report about how
the crocodiles had devoured
yet another careless man.

The boy thinks he would like to witness
                such an event.

But then, would he try
        to save the man?

He's not sure.

Or would he just watch
to see how a crocodile eats?

Would the man's legs go first
        or the arms
        or the stomach?

The boy imagines the lake
overpopulated with crocodiles
who never have enough to eat –
for he doesn't believe any fish
could live in such water.

There are hardly any trees
near the lake; no friendly monkeys
who would throw fruits down
to the crocodiles, as they do
        in one old story....

Kankaria Lake had also become
the most popular place
for suicides – That was a fact
which felt more like science-fiction
           to him.

On those Sunday afternoon
                family outings
he stops
in the middle of the bridge
and leans out
   towards the lake,
now and then sticking his legs out
through the railing
hoping at least one crocodile
will surface,
       raise its head.

But no.
Nothing ever happens.
Sometimes the wind pokes
the lake, making murky ripples.
But the crocodiles prefer
to remain hidden below.
How do they breathe?
      He worries.

In the end he was
always marched off
disappointed to the zoo
where he faced sullen animals
sometimes crouched far away
in the darkest part of the cage,
frightened in
   their festering skins.

A Different Way to Dance

1

It is June.
A record-breaking hot night.
Sizzling insects spatter against
the windshield as we drive
south from Boston.
My mother has stretched out
on the back seat.
Her eyes half closed, a little bored
her head begins to nod with sleep.

Then she sits up abruptly:

અરે પેલો હાથી જાય!

(aray paylo hathi jai!)

હાથી જાય!

(hathi jai!)

Hey, there goes an elephant!
An elephant's going by!
She shouts
pointing at the largest elephant I've ever seen –

chained inside an open truck.

He is a grey shadow
in a black truck, hurtling through
indigo New England night haze.

We look and look, desperately craning our necks,
wishing there were more light –
and we are not sure
whether we've actually seen
the expression in his eyes
or the delicate pink
curled inside the tip of his trunk.

There he goes
shuffling his feet
to his own Blues –
his trunk flies up to the right
to the left, extending the song,
                greeting the night air...

'Follow that truck!'
        My mother points,
'Follow that elephant!'

We follow him
as if he were the god,
        Ganesh himself.

2

Sometimes Parvati dreams
of her son's face:
the little boy Ganesh
who had greenish brown eyes –
huge eyes reminding her
of coriander leaves and sliced
ginger root floating in water
              in a deep wooden bowl.

Her little boy Ganesh
had a small nose, straight eyebrows,
thick knots of curly hair
before Shiva interfered.

Parvati even remembers the shape
of the newborn Ganesh she bore,
bent flower stalk elbows, the chest
                    flushing red –
the almost transparent skin
                    she first oiled
and the ripe melon soft fontanelle,
the spot she stroked everyday,
         always checking
just to be sure...

Sometimes the elephant head of Ganesh
dreams of the life among elephants it knew
before Shiva interfered.

How comfortable it was to walk
on four legs. To be able to speak with mountains,
to guess the mood of the wind...
and there was the jungle,
cool mud, dripping leaves,
the smell of wood – sandalwood, teak.
The smell of trees allowed to grow old
the smell of fresh water touched by deer
the smell of his newly found mate
the smell of their mounting passion –

None the less
everyday that elephant head of Ganesh
reveals a secret: a new way to eat,
another direction for language
a different way to dance...

In the early morning
        through greyish pink mist,
and in the evening
        through long shadows, smudged blue,
see how his one tusk balances those human knees,
how the elephant ears guide the human toes
until Parvati smiles
        Shiva steps aside,
and the elephant trunk sways
removing all that stands in the way –
the elephant trunk swings
                from side to side
hiding away the memory of Shiva's raised hand,
hiding away the knife-slashed soul,
that throbbing wound it carries
since leaving its first life.

Note:
Ganesh, the son of Shiva and Parvati, is the elephant-headed
god in Hindu mythology. He is a symbol for wisdom and pru-
dence. It is important to note that Ganesh did not always have
an elephant's head, but acquired one after Shiva through a mis-
understanding chopped off his original (human) head.

What Happened to the Elephant?

What happened to the elephant,
the one whose head Shiva stole
to bring his son Ganesh
                    back to life?

This is the child's curiosity
the nosy imagination that continues
probing, looking for a way
to believe the fantasy
a way to prolong the story.

If Ganesh could still be Ganesh
with an elephant's head,
then couldn't the body
                    of that elephant
find another life
with a horse's head – for example?

And if we found
a horse's head to revive
the elephant's body –
Who is the true elephant?
And what shall we do
about the horse's body?

Still, the child refuses
to accept Shiva's carelessness
and searches for a solution
without death.

        *   *   *

But now when I gaze
at the framed postcard
of Ganesh on my wall,
I also picture a rotting carcass
of a beheaded elephant
            lying crumpled up
on its side, covered with bird shit
vulture shit –

Oh that elephant
            whose head survived
for Ganesh –

He died, of course, but the others
in his herd, the hundreds
in his family must have found him.
They stared at him for hours
with their slow swaying sadness...
How they turned and turned
in a circle, with their trunks
facing outwards and then inwards
towards the headless one.

That is a dance
            a group dance
no one talks about.

Red August

Some days Jyoti's house smells
as if the walls had been washed
with *ghee* – butter melted inside out –
that is, butter strained through
                    a cheesecloth.
'It reeks. It stinks,' her children say,
offending Jyoti who sits
exhausted and shrivelled up
in a dark curtain-shielded corner,
unnoticed as a black spider
on a broken umbrella.

But today the sun pours in.
It is August. The monsoon
rains are coming to an end.
Now and then Jyoti pauses
to admire her hands – the henna has left
her palms stained dark
the colour of red-orange
red-brown earth
glistening like wet clay horses,
the ones from Kathiawad, from Kutch –
newly formed and soft.

Throughout the day
Jyoti stops in the middle
of every chore
to take a deep breath – and she smiles
as the henna scent grows.

All the women and the girls
in this neighbourhood
have filigreed serifs, miniature tapestries
of flowering vines spilling around
each finger, and tiny dots
for hummingbirds...

Why do they want this?
Not all of them are brides.
Some are little girls of four and five –
others, middle-aged women
sitting beside their teen-age daughters.
And all this
embroidery with henna mud
takes hours to complete
while they sit immobilized
with their palms outstretched.

But Jyoti doesn't care
for such designs. It's a waste
of time, she says,
slapping the henna paste
thick across her palms,
each fingernail hooded
because it's the *colour* she wants
            and the scent.

The scent of torn herbs
            and leafy plants
where animals have lain
hidden, licking their musky newborn...

Now Jyoti's hands are red blades
            swooping through the kitchen.

I was about to say
swooping down like birds
with impatient beaks

or like goldfish,
restless in someone's garden pond.

But that is not fair.
Her hands are
            more themselves.

Blistered, scratched – the skin
so raw for so long
that now she's used to the sting
of lemon, of salt.

Her hands look more
like the insides of muscles,

now her fist
looks more like her heart –

            open wounds

whipped horses
with twitching ears
now galloping
            now tearing across the grass –

Understanding The Ramayana

When they bowed
to us in their sparkling robes
I didn't want them to leave –

that day felt scorched
from the beginning;
unbearably hot
as if it were perpetually noon.

No cool imlee scented
                    Poona breeze,
so we had retreated
into the shadows cast
                    by our house.

We were tired, almost bored
when we saw them unfasten the latch
to the gate like thieves and slip through
into our garden before
anyone could stop them.

We were only children then
still we admired the fitted
yet comfortable sleeves
partly covering their furry arms –
arms which were a slightly different
                    brown from ours.

And I envied the tailor
who had stitched such earnest
headdresses – a tailor who
I thought was privileged to be
designing clothes for such creatures.

Sita, I stared at
        the longest.
She was so refined,
the way she folded up
her hands for *namaste*, while the slant
of her neck told us everything
about a disciplined suffering.
And the swift darting of her eyes
between Rama and Lakshman
required no words.

So it didn't matter
that none of them could speak.
We could even have done without
the whiny drone of the narrator
who also directed them, waving
his hands about with such force
as if that would sharpen
Sita's emotions.

It didn't matter
that now and then we glimpsed
a looped up tail
motionless as if drugged to sleep
beneath their costumes.

Their tails were fanned by swishing hems
when they leaped –
Sita flying away in fear;
Rama flying in for a fight
        to save her.

Bright pink and orange frills
speckled with blue-green sequins
and outlined with silver
threads, zig-zagging stars –
bright frills would flutter up
revealing the quiet tail – its power

dormant and forbidden to take any part
in the actions of Prince Rama
                    or Princess Sita.

We felt relieved to know
the narrator hadn't chopped off
or even shortened
the glorious question marks
curling behind their backs.

Only Hanuman
allowed to use his tail
was the most joyous
and felt perfectly cast.

Monkeys more humane
                    than anyone –
But it relieved me to see
a flash of pride, of anger
cut through their meek faces.
Or was it only acting?

Where had they been found?
And how had they learnt
the meaning of *The Ramayana*
                    that well?

So absorbed were we
as if we had never heard
this saga before,
that we didn't mind
the withered, small-pox
                    scarred face
of the man who owned them;
we didn't pay much attention
to the chains around the delicate
                    monkey feet – preventing them
from jumping very far.

In the end our only regret
was that we couldn't join them
when they were dragged away
by their worn out master.

We stood in the middle
                of the garden
watching them leave –
our hands hanging limp
        by our sides.

They seemed to disappear
into haloes of swirling dust.

The gate clanged shut
        and the heat
descended like a curtain
forcing us back
        into the shade.

Devibhen Pathak

1

How did the tea taste
        that morning?
Was she nervous?
Or was it a simple decision,
something that had to be done?

The girl gulps down
her milk this morning.
She is twelve-years-old.
It is 1938. One day
she'll be my mother –
But for now she watches
her own mother get dressed.

I imagine my grandmother, Devibhen Pathak,
praying as always to Govinda,
her little brass Krishna
                forever solid
forever the playful child
she bathed and dressed every day.
Devibhen's forehead stays cool
with a brown paste of sandalwood.
Was she quiet that day?
Was she worried?

ચાલ, ચાલ! સપાટ પહેરી લે!

(chaal, chaal! Sapat payhri lay!)
Let's go! Put on your slippers!
She must have said
even in those days using the word
        sapat
adapted from the Portugese.

I imagine the Ahmedabad sun, salty
on the T.B. coughed up
            spittle stained, betel nut leaf slimy streets –
A city where the water
still tastes salty;
land that was once beneath the sea.

Now it is 1938.
Devibhen has decisions to make.
Decisions about money she didn't have,
about a small lump of gold she inherited,
gold she wanted worked into a necklace...
It was a way to give
the gold a more useful shape.
Something to present to her daughter
when she came of age.
Something for her daughter's daughter's daughter...
The design had to be chosen,
the shape of the links on the chain –
and finally, the shape of the pendant.
What should the ruby define?

She imagined this necklace of deep
yellow gold, warm around the neck
and heavy as a small snake, the links
are chiselled grains of rice
        carved full and geometrically rounded
to catch the sort of shadows
a snake's spine would invite.

She who understood snakes,
who respected cobras and would lead
them away from her garden with a prayer
            and a burning lantern;
this wise woman, my grandmother
must have remembered snakes
while she spoke with the goldsmith.

And then she had to choose
a shape for the pendant.
She didn't hesitate, my mother reports,
for her it was clearly the geometric sun,
a wheel for life and luck,
a four-petalled flower
twisting out of a circle, in turn encircled
by a hexagon – for her
it was clearly the sacred swastika
that only appears in red. She had it
held together with a ruby
to remind us of the goodness within red.

But it is 1938
and the goldsmith reminds her
of the latest news:

અરે બ્હેન, તમને ખબર નથી . . . ?
(aray bhen, tamnay khabar nathi...?)

Oh bhen, don't you know...?

Still she didn't hesitate,
my mother shows me with a look
how she dismissed his worries with her faith.

And in the heart of Devibhen's mind
snakes moved, bluish black
darting through the grass –
and in the mind of Devibhen's heart
wheels turned
but the swastika remained sacred,
beloved,
untouched by history.
Who was Hitler? Mahatma Gandhi
                        was her daily news,
                            her truth.

2

She was right
and she was wrong.
Why else do I keep this necklace
in a box? Why else
am I suddenly unable to wear
this yellow gold snake heavy symbol?
I'm unable to believe the swastika
is untouched by history.

I remember practicing drawing swastikas
as a child, with other children...
we also practiced drawing circles
and squares, perfect triangles
and five pointed stars.

Triangular Parvati
          pointing earthward.
Triangular Shiva
          pointing skyward.

Their bodies, sharp –
pared down to pure form.
Is that where truth lies?
In the shadow of a shoulder blade,
the corner of a triangle?

But the swastikas were always in red
and as I drew them
I always thought
this is holy
          holy
          holy – as I tried to steady my hand
always believing there was pure goodness
branching out from the centre.

I remember drawing swastikas everywhere
in so many notebooks, and outside
            even in the mud –
thinking this is beauty
this is true wisdom – while the difficult circles
and stars filled the background.

What does a circle mean?
What does a triangle mean?
Who knows the true meanings?

Oh didn't I love the Hindu swastika?
And later, one day didn't I start wishing
I could rescue that shape from history?

But how shall I begin?
What shall I say?
            Oh my German-born daughter,
            innocent girl with a Lübecker
            Baltic-eyed innocent father...

Look at those neat rows of swastikas
                        in red
plastered across the temple grounds, look
at the swastikas framing every wedding invitation.
The dowry determines
the paper's quality
the quality of the print.
Even that motion of the hand, that gesture
sweeping across the temple floor
is not always holy, not always innocent.
Something is wrong:
So many old religions fatten
on arguments, on fresh murders
or do they call that offerings?
Someone's blood, someone's money
someone's wife, someone's son
should not have been touched.

Meanwhile, the shape of the swastika remains:
Hakenkreuz, fylfot,
and when you slant your head
                    towards the sun
also St Brigid's plaited fancy cross...
And my daughter born
on the first of February,
                    the first day of an early Springtide...

स्वस्ति, स्वस्ति

(swasti, swasti,)   they used to say

meaning: Be well, be well!

Oh my German-born daughter,
arriving during a spell of bright Spring weather –
                    lucky girl
                    to be born on St Brigid's day...
What will you say? What colours will you
prefer? In what language
                    will you speak?

II

Angels' Wings

Angels' Wings

I can recall that age
very well: fourteen-years-old,
when I thought I understood
Lenin and Mao,
and Christina Rossetti was beginning
to sound silly.

One April Saturday morning
after swimming lessons
I stood waiting for my father,
pacing the formaldehyde
            stung corridor,
I twirled equidistant between
the autopsy room and his office.

My eleven-year-old brother
                and I together
but silent for a quarter of an hour
as if all that swimming, all that chlorine
had altered our breathing
had washed away our speech.

A heavy door opened and a man,
dark as the shadows he cast,
a man with electric white hair
asked us to step inside.
There was something
he wanted us to see.

The room was festooned with wings,
all of a similar shape
            and strangely human.
Perhaps fairies' wings
            or angels' wings, I thought,
made of real gossamer...

As we stepped closer
we could see clumps of clogged cells,
those grape-like clusters meant to blossom with oxygen –
now shrivelled
beside rivers of blood choked black.

They were not drawings,
not photographs –
but human lungs
well-preserved by someone's
skill in histology.
He could tell us how old
their owners had lived to be
for how many years each had smoked.
He would tell us everything
except their names.

Twenty pairs of lungs
pinned up on his wall:
a collage of black and grey,
here and there some chalky yellow
                    some fungus-furred green.

How long did we stand there?
And what did we say?
I don't remember eating lunch
or what we did
for the rest of that day –
Only those twenty pairs of nameless lungs,
the intimate gossamer
of twenty people I never knew
lungless in their graves.

Mozartstrasse 18

for Eleanor Wilner, who first asked me
to describe post-war Bremen

I am sitting in the *Spielplatz*
around the corner from Mozartstrasse
wondering
where guilt ends
and where it begins;
while the children dig in the sandbox
and the sixteen-month-old boy
I'm looking after, pours sand
onto my lap.
I don't see how guilt
could possibly begin here.

And yet,
there are buildings in Bremen
I can't help considering evil.

And there is this dream
that does not leave me –
beginning gently one night
with me going downstairs, out
of the house,
my hand on the rain-dripping gate –
that's when I see them:
They are all there,
an international crowd
all dressed exquisitely in black and white,
full flowing black coats
a glimpse of white linen collars...
Their presence makes the damp morning
warmer, the air
takes on the smell of fresh coffee
and chocolate from their clothes.

They walk slowly, just like tourists
with plenty of time.
They come up the adjoining street
towards Mozartstrasse, towards me
while I stand by the gate.
Not a word is spoken
but they all greet me and point
to this house, number 18.
They greet me with their eyes
full of questions, there is something
they want to ask me, but I cannot guess
what it is. Not a word is spoken
but they all stare deep into my eyes,
separately
each with his own questions,
each with her own questions.

I remember all their eyes, all dark,
dark, but each with a different darkness,
a field of dark flowers
and tree trunks completely covered
with hundreds of dark butterflies...
that's when I first try
to speak, to move,
to say at least 'hello'.
But I can't.

I continue staring into their calm eyes
fresh and clear
as if they all had had a good night's sleep.
And I think, how strange, as I stand
fixed by the gate,
they seem to know me, how strange
that they don't speak and why are they pointing
at this house?

Mozartstrasse 18. Is it important?
Does it matter where we live,
what happened before?
I wonder
while the children dig in the sandbox
and the sixteen-month-old boy
I'm looking after, pours sand
onto my lap.

It is one thing to know
what happened before
but quite another to read the list
of names, of streets, of houses...
It is one thing to know
what happened before
but quite another to live here today
and to find out precisely who lived where
in 1937, 1938...To look through
the original *Bremer Adressbuch*, complete with advertisements,
and then to follow up with 1983 statistics.
Who was arrested, shot.
Who got sent to Minsk, who escaped...

For example, the Ries family
who lived at Mozartstrasse 25,
Albert and Emma with their two children,
Günther and Cäcilie, left for the United States
on the thirteenth of December 1938.
Their house is no longer here.

But number 18 remains a mystery.
Theodor Gruja, *Damenschneider*
lived here, with his shop upstairs.
There are five other tenants
in this building, listed in 1937.
This building of 1854, where
I feel so free with these four metre high ceilings,
tall windows everywhere to let in the light.
The perfect place for a tailor,
I tell the landlady as we sit on the balcony
trying to guess what happened to Theodor Gruja.
Over coffee and cake she tells me
about the thousands of needles
she found all over the floors, pins and needles;
about his Jewish wife
sent away to America. *Thousands of needles*
she repeats, and pins even stuck in the walls.
That was 1975, she says, when she bought
and restored the building, saving it from demolition.
Thousands of needles, and no toilets, she says
pointing to the spot in the garden
where the outhouses had been.

Why so many pins even stuck
in the walls?
I see rivers of needles streaming silver
paths from one room into another –
Who threw everything
onto the floor? Who took the sewing machines?
Who took the clothes? I see rivers full
of needles, flickering wet gills,
and in a shifting
trick of sunlight they could be
just hatched salmon I watch from a cliff top,
smelt lashing silver trails.

It is April now
and the huge sprawling chestnut tree
has small leaves,
small as a six-month-old baby's hands.
We talk about the tailor's Jewish wife
and I look at the tree
with an impatient tightness in my legs,
knowing it was here for all those years –
as if I could blame it, let alone
question it…
Now there are these lengthening days:
April, May, June, the chestnut leaves grow larger,
and our rooms are filled with so much light,
so I can't stop thinking
about Theodor Gruja, *Damenschneider*,
and his wife.

Yellow October

in memory of Herta Blieffert (1907-1986)

A tree can become like that only in New England's fall,
in Iowa's fall...
Not in Europe's autumn.

This maple made its own light:
clear yellow
as if its sap were singing,
smouldering alert
and preparing itself for something beyond winter.

Of course, I thought it was the moon at first –
but the moon was a sharp bitten off
punky earring that night.
There were no street lamps
and the wide Iowa houses stayed heavily dark
with their 2:00 a.m. privacy.
So the tree made its own light
as if preparing itself to speak.

A tree can become like that only in New England's fall,
in Iowa's fall...
Not in Europe's autumn.

This clear yellow light
made me want to stand there
beside it all night, just staring up the trunk.
And it even felt warm there, so I thought
I could easily sleep beneath
the saxifrage-amber,
lively bright leaves, clean and inquiring
as a young giraffe's wet eyes.
I wanted to sleep beside that strength,
to sleep with that tree, that yellow –

Wine from Bordeaux

Today I've invented a man
who has bought two thousand bottles
of a 1985 wine from Bordeaux,
the *Bois-Malot* which won
the Bronze medal in 1986.
And now this 1985 *Bois-Malot* has become
even better than gold, and it will stay
good, it will delight you
            for years to come.

Over here, in Ostertor
you and I would have to pay
about *vierzehn Mark* for a bottle.
But I'm sure my imaginary man
has worked out some special deal
with the shopkeepers, maybe even
with the people
            who planted the grapes.

He's bought two thousand bottles already
and plans to buy more.

1985 is the year
before Chernobyl.

He doesn't like
to ingest anything harvested
                        in Europe after 1985.

'This wine goes very well
with New Zealand lamb,'
he confides to the wine shop owner.
'It's the only meat
I feel safe eating...' he whispers.

No doubt
he's got a large cellar
to hoard all those bottles
of crimson Bordeaux
with their handsome brown labels.
I imagine him smiling
at their sharp dark winks –
      rows and rows of rounded shadows
each time he opens the door.

There's another man
I can tell you about.
He is real.
He got himself sterilized
in May 1986 when he was eighteen
because he was convinced
his chromosomes were damaged.
And he didn't want to pass on
      any mistakes.

While the women
who gave birth over here
in 1986 sometimes didn't know
      what to eat.

I imagine some of them still
scrutinize their children
with fear, wishing they could supervise
the health of every cell.

While in the towns near Chernobyl
embryos didn't make it
fetuses didn't make it
and the babies who managed
to get born and who managed to grow
into children – suddenly
become sick with leukemia.

But the child
that I still think of
was one eight-year-old boy
who loved playing in the sand
      like most children
who didn't notice dirt or mud on his clothes
      like most children –

But then he started begging
to be allowed to take a shower
whenever he came indoors
thinking the water
      thinking the water would wash
          it all off –

A Story for Pearse

But the more fragrant body,
the body that was love, rose up,
no rot as yet set in,
evicted the people from the wake,
and raced out the door
after the soul that had been so faithful,
and fell, by the lake's edge, without
seeing the soul again.

None of the mourners was there
to bury either body.

– Pearse Hutchinson, 'The Soul that Kissed the Body'

Reading your new book today
I am reminded of my great-aunt,
of her soul, her body...
How she died alone
with a terrible stench
oozing from her body –
how almost no one mourned her.

Oh the lucky Soul
that felt moved to kiss life,
to kiss the Body before departing!

But your version, your lines
seem also written for her –
and all day your words with their urgent movement
have been pulling my mind
back to my great-aunt.

My great-aunt Hirabhen
was rescued from her mother-in-law
rescued from her husband
soon after she was married.

Her mother-in-law used to beat her
with a bamboo pole.
She made her work all day
with little food,
then whipped her every night
until her pretty skin turned ugly.

At least they didn't pour kerosene over her head,
at least they didn't set her ablaze.

But who knows what finally compelled
the young woman Hirabhen to tell her parents
     in those days
to go to a court of law
where the judge said:
'This is no marriage! You are free!
You can choose again,
you can decide for yourself –'

She chose to become a nurse
to earn her own money.
She said she wanted
          to learn something new
to help others.

But I am certain
that her soul walked out
on her that day in court.
After the battle was won
there was nothing more
for the soul to say –
after she was free
she could never feel her soul again.

The soul was gone
        to the lake
in a forest where no one
        could follow.

She had a life full
of naked bodies – diseased
patients broken with bedsores
and married doctors who enjoyed
          lying with her
enjoyed tricking her
into believing anything.

Then, for a long time
there was always a different man
invariably weird and coarse
compared to her delicate face.

What was it she searched for in the body?
In the blood cells, the plasma, the hair,
the eyes, the eye-lids –
In the length of a scar...
Was it the way to recognize death
          from far away?
The way death flings its own light
          around a body
unmistakeably marking it?
The medicine? The dosage? The numbers?
Numbers defining fevers,
chemicals, hours, years...

What was it she wanted to learn?

The time it takes
          for stitches to heal?
The time it takes
          for a scar to fade?

But I am certain
she could never feel her soul,
          her self.

It was easy for everyone to say
she should have found God
like her older sister
who was happily married and blessed
                    with children.

It was easy for everyone
to say *what* she should have done.
And, no doubt, they thought
she had done something
to deserve her fate.

I wonder if she ever
spoke to God.
I imagine she would have given up
with a Lord who allows torture.
And how would she have continued
believing in a God who dwells
in every heart? The Lord
in her mother-in-law's heart?
The Lord in her husband's heart?

Towards the end
when she was truly old
and I had just stopped
            being a child – and I had just been told
about her life –
I was afraid of her paranoia
afraid of her frantic-caged-animal-fear,
her disjointed spat out speech
            I couldn't follow.

What did flowers mean to her?
And colours?
And birdsong?
How bird shadows screech
chopping up the tropical light –
Did she care?

What did children mean to her?
Sometimes I think my mother,
her patient niece, was the only
person, the only child
who ever consoled her.

Towards the end
when she was dying
(and my mother was not informed)
she used to gaze at herself
naked in the mirror
arching her back, head tilted
in a way that once was coy.
Did she see
her cracked smelly skin?

Did she have a more fragrant body,
a second body that was love?

Towards the end
when she was dying
she used to poke her naked chest
with a tired finger
as if to say *here   here*
this is where
            my soul used to be.

Note:

The quotation is the title poem from Pearse Hutchinson's
collection, *The Soul that Kissed the Body* (Oldcastle, Co.
Meath: The Gallery Press, 1990).

Groningen: Saturday Market on a Very Sunny Day

The large eye was still fresh,
perfectly intact: the size of a cow's eye
and the iris, black.
Clean black against the white eyeball.
Oh who will buy this fish-head
with a cow's eye?
The eye remained stuck while looking up
at the nets, at the surface of the water,
at the shadows cast by the bottom of the boat...
or after being yanked in
it looked up at the sky, the knife,
at the blank face of the busy fisherman –
it looked up
with the lethargic sadness of cows
and the Renaissance emotions of praying peasants.

One by one, at different times,
the six of us separate in the crowds,
distracted at every corner
by something new – one by one
this afternoon at different times
somehow we all saw
this particularly thick fish-head
with a sad cow's eye.
And in the evening, simultaneously
we all started to speak of it.
'Oh who will buy, who would dare buy
that fish-head?' we wondered during supper –
unable to say more.
We were strangely thirsty.
Thirsty, thirsty,
that night
we couldn't drink enough.

Counting Sheep White Blood Cells

for Jo Shapcott

It was like being ordered
                    to count the stars
and to classify them
by their size, their brightness –

And it was like being ordered
to count all the tiny wild flowers
in a never-ending field
            and to name them –

There were days
when she, the lab technician
would sit staring through the microscope
for five hours straight
counting sheep white blood cells.

It didn't put her to sleep.
Instead, it made her eyes feel powerful,
it made her feel wired
as if she were the source
of electricity for that microscope.

Whenever she looked up
to put in a new slide
the lab whirled
            unreal around her
for she had gone with all her dreams
into the galaxies of sheep.

It was the macrophage she wanted,
the one cell that doesn't grow
in vitro – her missing secret
to understanding
the immune system.
But she had to count
and yet discount the lymphocytes
and leukocytes and the large
erythrocytes getting in the way.

And they were beautiful
strangely rounded flowers, these corpuscles,
some fuzzy dandelions
      gone to seed
but still intact, translucent
balls of cotton –
Some prickly burrs
      stuck fast together
so she can't forget
the sheep, the tangled wool
full of rain and grass...
Some fuzzy dandelions
gone to seed – but there was
no time to admire them.

Across the street
      in the hospital where
she also worked, people tried to live
with cancer.

She was eighteen
and always kept her notebook handy.
A notebook full of numbers, drawings...
entire pages crossed out
      leading nowhere.
At the end of the day
she would feel so numb.

That was a time of living
in a different vocabulary:
laboratory Latin.
But also: *we've sacrificed the animals.*
We've harvested the cells.

That is how
she started to speak.

The Mad Woman in the Attic

for Hartmut Eïng

The mad woman in the attic
has a new machine by her bed.

Once she thought of becoming a mermaid
but now she knows her destiny
is to become a black right whale.

I have read that
Black right whales
have comparatively small flippers
and large tail flukes,
but no dorsal fin...

Die dulle Schwester
you call her,
meaning *die tolle, die verrückte* –
meaning the mad, the deranged sister.
And you give me her red scarf
with yellow polka dots.

I have read that
When feeding, this whale usually stays below
for about fifteen minutes,
then surfaces to breathe
five or six times in rapid succession,
rolling
just below the surface
between each breath.

The machine churns all night
all day, making gasping sounds
it alters the cells in her lungs, turns
her blood into whale blood.

About black right whales
someone once wrote:
It is a stupid, blundering beast
that appears to cause harm only by mistake
and when in its death throes.

At first you don't believe me
and show me how people leave
their homes to greet
a real black whale
        stranded in the snow.
This is the future, centuries after
the inevitable nuclear war.
They carry sticks and stumble
like children just learning to walk.
They look at the whale like children
seeing a large animal for the first time.

Is it worship, is it love,
is it fear, is it wonder
glittering in their eyes?

The mad woman in the attic
wants to be greeted like that.

How long will it take
before she's gone? And how
will she go? Will she leap through
the window, then arching her spine
fling herself into the harbour
before she's a full grown whale?
Or, will she grow indoors
brooding revenge until one day
the roof splinters open, the house crashes
down, and is dragged away
with her into the sea...

I don't know.
But her rosy face
          round as a baby's
doesn't fool me –

Notes:
This poem refers obliquely to various paintings by
Hartmut Eing.
The italicized lines are quotations from Ivan T. Sander-
son, *Follow the Whale* (New York: Bramhall House, 1956).

The Fish Hat

1

For weeks this is how
she has been dreaming of herself.

So far, she can manage
to imagine shadows
draped over her scooped out parts.

Her dream shadows mimic the shape
her flesh used to take
before the surgery.

But the shadows are blue
as if she were a Hindu god,
                    a divine hermaphrodite –

Yellow edged with red
clings to her neck and wrists.
It's the sort of yellow one sees on signs
warning of radioactivity –

And there are holes
you can see right through;
holes, where her nipples used to be.

Her hands are young
are knotted together into a tight ball
                    hanging pear-shaped...

Her face looks like a cutting board
as if some intern had practiced on it.

There's a fish hat she designed
herself long ago when she was twelve:
Homage to a baked fish, ready to eat
complete with fork and knife
and a thick slice of lemon.
A fish hat that has turned
as blue as her own shadows;
a fish hat that now seems glued
to her head through all these dreams
after the surgery.

2

It almost looked like something
that had come out of the sea.

But I had never seen
                an opaque jellyfish
with a single, round, closed eye-lid.

They brought it over in a rush
first thing in the morning
the nurse running with the styrofoam box
padded with ice. 'This is not my job!'
I wanted to say.
'You are supposed to dig out the tumours
yourself. What happened to the surgeon?'
I wondered. But I didn't speak.
I was afraid my voice would break –
afraid my voice would affect my hands...

I had to make an incision into the centre
and watch the sphere collapse.

The movement must feel like pulling out the calyx
                              of a large flower
of a fully blossomed rose
one doesn't want to destroy –
then watching the petals scatter –

except that I had to consider the blood,
I had to try
to cut out a segment
of a tumour without blood. I had to spend
the rest of the day analysing that tumour.

3

After Picasso painted her
                    he laughed.
It was a big joke.
He showed her off
to all his friends... At least
this is what you think.
As we stand in the museum
you picture them *once upon a time*
drinking litres of red wine, toasting her
surrounding her hollow blue shadows
and laughing, laughing
especially at the fish hat.

Note:

This poem refers to Pablo Picasso's painting, *Femme assise au chapeau poisson* (Sitting woman with fish hat), 1942.

The Echoes in Poona

One day the pure, clean rhesus monkeys
gagged on the sun,
on their half-eaten ripe fruits,
and now their screams for Hanuman*
echo through the jungle
as they spit out the moon, the stars...
If you look closely
you can see where
the nets have left marks
across their thin fingers.

They shake their heads
trying to dislodge
the grinding noise of jeep tires
on dirt roads.
Their tails still expect
to brush against leaves, grass...
and their neck muscles
are not used to this sudden
lack of wind.

From our garden,
when I stand near the bougainvillaea
I can hear their caged cries
echoing, echoing – freshly torn
from the heart of the jungle.
They shy away from the wires,
at first they even flinch
from each other.
They are wild with rage
echoing, echoing –

After a few days
they are quiet, a young mother
turns to stroke her sister,
a louse is found, removed. Soon
their fingers work to search each other –
They take their time, such gentle care,
as they reinvent their family.

Such pure, clean rhesus monkeys,
uncontaminated specimens:
Forced helpers in the search
for vaccinations and antibiotics.

Meanwhile the men who watched the hunt
from their small tents
are now busy focusing microscopes.
My father also
spends his days counting
monkey kidney cells in vitro.
He scrubs his hands
until they bleed, until the skin
starts peeling. He bathes
several times a day
while colleagues less careful
die from the disease.

From our garden
I can see the back of the building:
rows of air conditioners
drone against the noise
of the new rhesus monkeys.
One day my six-year-old brother begins
a new game
where he visits the monkeys
and feeds them flowers, lost in his game
he gives them branches with berries
while the tired watchman,
skinny Satnarayan, almost dozes –

And my tired father, lost in thought
in his windowless room
examines test tubes,
his eyes straining against
the fluorescent lights.

Years pass.
Microscopes improve.
My father will soon retire.
These days, when my year-old daughter
wants something
from the kitchen table,
from the shelves, her arms thrusting out
like a trapeze artist,
her urgent *hu hu hu* speech
reminds me of those monkeys – and last week
when she cried hot with fever
and tense with antibiotics
I lay sleepless through 5:00 a.m.
remembering the bold black eyes
of the caged baby monkeys
eager with surprise as they pulled
on sap-wet weeds with berries
offered by my brother –
their dark velvet fingers grasping for
the bruised yellow and bruised red
velvet fruit.

* Hanuman: The monkey god in Hindu mythology.

Walking Across the Brooklyn Bridge, July 1990

In New York
children are being shot
to death this summer.
It's usually an accident.
Someone else, no doubt an adult,
was meant to be killed instead.
It's not a war,
just a way to settle disagreements.

Walking across the Brooklyn Bridge
one feels removed from everything
as if one were passing by
in a low flying plane.
Below, on both sides the cars
stream by. Above, the steel
cables converge, tighten.
The muscles in my legs feel
exposed, worn out.

The children somehow get in
the way: They're found dead
in the car, in the house,
in the crib. Sometimes it happens
that the father
was cleaning the gun.

Walking across the Brooklyn Bridge
today I see work being done.
Repairs. Clean, clear-cut
adjustments. Renovation.
The humming of steel against wind
drills through my bones –
it's driven up my spine.
The humming does not end.

But the worst case
I read about didn't involve a gun.
Simply a father, newly arrived from Montana
who decided to feed
his six-day-old son
to a hungry German Shepherd.
Was the mother really asleep?

Walking across the Brooklyn Bridge
I pause, look around.
What is real in this symbol,
in that other one over there...?
The steel cables have become a cage,
a sanctuary. Whose cage?
Whose hope?

In another section
of the newspaper I read
about the ever growing problems of refugees.
Who will take them in?
Especially the ones from Vietnam,
a favourite subject for photographers:
flimsy boats, someone's thin arm in the way –
Who can forget those eyes?
And who can judge those eyes
                    that vision?

Walking across the Brooklyn Bridge
even on a hot afternoon
one sees many joggers.
And there is the view, of course.

Looking across the water
I think of those people from Vietnam.
The mothers, the fathers,
what they wouldn't have given,
what they would still give –
their blood, their hair, their livers, their kidneys,
their lungs, their fingers, their thumbs –
to get their children
past the Statue of Liberty.

III

Until Our Bones Prevent Us
from Going Further

The Sea at Night

for Michael

The sea at night, all black
yet distinguishable from the sky, all black.
Close above the sea: a vertical sickle
a flame yellow waxing moon –
and right above the moon:
a chrysanthemum yellow star,
the evening star.

All in a straight line –
so we wondered if this happens
every night or once a century,
we wondered while

the sea swayed, the sky shifted
the moon turned, the star slipped

and there was no time
for a photograph –
       no time, so we watched
               sleepless through the night,
unable to lie still
unable to stop talking...

Another Portrait of Bartolo

for Esther, who gave me the first portrait

Fishermen don't swim in the sea.
They say it would be so frivolous,
they say it brings bad luck.
Bartolo, for example, walks in
towards his boat – still praying.
He wades in everyday
                    fully dressed for work.
Over here
the sun always hangs above the water,
the sun is always on Bartolo's face.

Today
Bartolo sits with his back to us.
I watch him. He plays cards this afternoon
instead of getting his boat ready.

Short, muscular and slightly hunchbacked,
devout, superstitious,
thick grey hair beneath his cap,
he stands out in his blue
and white plaid shirt.
The others, his crew,
are sitting with him – playing cards
instead of ploughing the waves.

This is one of the last
sunny days in October.
Bartolo's movements are
the sharpest. He slams
his hand down again and again.
I keep turning to look.
The others are quiet.
They are all old men,
and I wonder who will fish

the way they do ten years from now.
Who will fish setting out from this beach
with nets thrown out of a small boat?

A little girl shouts 'Bartolo! Bartolo!'
The sun is so hot
one could swim for an hour in the sea.
But Bartolo's boat
lies far up on the shore
as if he expected a storm.
The others, his crew,
disappointed no doubt,
remain quiet.

So Bartolo ignores the sea
this afternoon, while I squint
at the five o'clock glitter.
Later, when the sun is red
and almost swallowed up,
I see Bartolo has finished his game.
For once he's not pulling the nets in
at this hour, his cap dodging the orange glare.
Now he rises abruptly from the table
and for once with his back to the setting sun
enters Francisco's Bar.

Rooms by the Sea

for Michael

It's summer all right.
This light makes me think
of June in Miami
July in Ocean City
August in Cape Cod.

This heat reminds me of a certain freedom
this light is the colour of a certain freedom
we had one summer –
the freedom to want
a child, the longing to let life go on
                              as it pleases.

The heat has flung the door wide open –
and the light is constant.
The cry of our imaginary child
breaks our afternoon nap,
untangles our sticky thighs...
The sea is a loud salty glitter
pounding against the shore, back and forth
back and forth, as if driven by nervous fishes.
The light remains steady
                              and the heat is constant –

Someone, we don't see,
has stepped inside
and walks through the kitchen, that we don't see.
I imagine you
            grabbing a beer
        from the fridge.

The sofa burns red
the carpet crackles green
and the picture in the pine wood frame
is fading away.

Note:

This poem refers to Edward Hopper's painting,
Rooms by the Sea, 1951.

Franz Marc's *Blaue Fohlen*

I want to meet
Franz Marc's blue foals.
I see them in a secluded field
in a place like Kentucky or Dublin.
They make the morning glories miserable
as they run through the blue grass of Kentucky,
they make the morning glories miserable
as they run through the endless wet
June blue-gold light of Dublin.
I want to find their blue ears
and unravel some riddles.
I want to nose their blue necks.

Sunlight in a Cafeteria

1

The man thinks:
'What a lousy deal.
It'll take all day to fix that car.
I wish the heat would let up.
The kids will want to go
to the beach again.
I don't have the time for it.
Who'll paint the house?'

2

Meanwhile, at the other table,
                    the woman thinks:
'It's July again.
What a month to spend in New York City.
What a month to be pregnant.
Why do they call it morning sickness
when it hits me in the afternoon as well?

And sometimes even at night .
when I least suspect it.
This dress is already a bit tight
for me. I wish Jim would hurry up.
Can't stand the smell of that guy's cigarette.
Should I have another coffee?
I hope Jim likes my hair.
I didn't know New York would be
like this. I'm not ready for it.
July used to be my favourite month.
Always sunny. I'm glad I'm not in Denmark anymore.
I probably shouldn't sit in the sun
but I missed it so much over there.

I like this New York
July sunlight, it's so honest –
right to the point,
no misunderstandings.
I know where I stand.'

Note:

This poem refers to Edward Hopper's painting,
Sunlight in a Cafeteria, 1958.

Portrait of a Double Portrait

She has just eaten mushrooms and celery
fried with onions and soy sauce,
and there's a green haze around her eyes.

She is growing a new face:
broader forehead, larger eyes...
while her new hair simply grows longer.
Look at the sharp light,
the crisp shadows around her new nose.
Is it confusing?
How her skin glistens and itches
as if lavender were growing
out of her pores...
out of this canvas.

She will keep her old face
tucked inside her smile.
She is Persephone
learning to become Demeter.
She only counts in weeks now,
and says she's twenty-nine weeks pregnant.
She always thinks of food,
especially apples and sprouted beans.
She is growing a second face
and when the fetus inside her kicks
the haze around her eyes grows greener.

Note:
This poem refers to Eugène Brands' painting, *Dubbel portret van zwangere vrouw* (Double Portrait of a Pregnant Woman).

White Asparagus

Who speaks of the strong currents
streaming through the legs, the breasts
of a pregnant woman
in her fourth month?

She's young, this is her first time,
she's slim and the nausea has gone.
Her belly's just starting to get rounder
her breasts itch all day,

and she's surprised that what she wants
is *him*
     inside her again.
Oh come like a horse, she wants to say,
move like a dog, a wolf,
               become a suckling lion-cub –

Come here, and here, and here –
but swim fast and don't stop.

Who speaks of the green coconut uterus
the muscles sliding, a deeper undertow
and the green coconut milk that seals
her well, yet flows so she is wet
from his softest touch?

Who understands the logic
behind this desire?

Who speaks of the rushing tide
                    that awakens
her slowly increasing blood –?
And the hunger
            raw obsessions beginning
with the shape of asparagus:
sun-deprived white and purple-shadow-veined,
she buys three kilos
of the fat ones, thicker than anyone's fingers,
she strokes the silky heads,
some are so jauntily capped...
            even the smell pulls her in –

Distances

Once in the ocean over here
in Conil, at the outskirts of Europe –
once I'm in and swimming
in this pocket
of the Atlantic Ocean,
every place feels closer:

Africa, America,
you are not far away.
I touch you through the waves
simultaneously –

One day Africa sends the wind called *levante*,
the next day the Americas send fish.
Meanwhile the waves rush back and forth,
crashing north and south
east and west
depending on the wind.
And every place slides through
my fingers with the frothy
just breaking waves, relentless
salty water.

Inland again, it's different.
All is separate, distant.
The atlas fills my mind
with its many borders, and this ocean
lies trapped on the page
like a gasping beached whale.

The Rooster in Conil

I like the size
        of the windows,
two feet by three feet.
Over here in Spain
one needs a place to escape
from the sun.

I like the bars on the windows.
Are they made of iron?
The bars and the window sills feel
as if some one had pulled them off
my grandfather's house in Bhavnagar
and stuck them on this whitewashed house by the sea.

Outside my bedroom window
there's a sprawled out bush
of night blooming white flowers,
the addicting fragrance fingers my sleep,
tricks my nose into believing I'm home.

And in the background, accompanying everyone
there's the hush-hush constant
swishing whipped up sound of the sea...

What do the bars on the windows keep out?
Dogs? Cats? Thieves?
Or Alfonsa's never tiring rooster
who begins crowing at 3:00 a.m.
as if the sun would rise early just for him.
He could be Don Quixote's messenger
the way he continues
announcing something that must be
eating up his heart,
the way he continues all day
                until the sun has gone.

And in the background, accompanying everyone
there's the sound of the sea.

All this crowing has affected,
maybe enhanced this rooster's voice.
I too wake up at 3:00 a.m.
wondering if it's my eight-month-old daughter
who often sounds
            like a sad saxophone.
There's a bit of Van Morrison sometimes
in her stretched out lilting plea.
Other times, I hear a bit of Tom Waits
in her sudden call.
How she mimics the music she became
attached to before
            she was born.

And in the background, accompanying everyone
there's the sound of the sea.

Is it my daughter?
Is it the rooster?
Is it some very talented musician
who is in love and wants
to try out a new tune on his saxophone?

And in the background, accompanying everyone
there's the sound of the sea.

My child is asleep.
And so I stare at the bars
            on the windows, at the sky,
remembering similar birds, similar sounds
from Bhavnagar, similar days
when mornings started
            with animals clamouring
before the sun had a chance.

Just White Chips

These seashells aren't even beautiful.
Just white chips
the colour of angry work day breakfasts
full of the news and no one to talk to.
Just sharp pieces
with the sound of exasperated eggshells
from bored hens.

These seashells aren't even beautiful.
And yet I hold them
as if to comfort them,
loving them only because
I found them between spinach gumboed seaweed
and giant lychee jellyfish
while I ran between thunderstorms
along the Baltic Sea; wanting them only
because of a certain day at a certain place.

Beyond Edinburgh

for the Austyns

Travelling
along the eastern shore
beyond Edinburgh
beyond the Firth of Forth
blinding fields of rapeseed
flash through the clattering train windows.
The diesel fumes make me dizzy
but the colour revives me,
keeps me surprised.
Such brightness! Almost artificial yellow
like spilt paint in this land of damp greyish
blues and musty duns
overshadowing whatever is green.

Another time,
travelling the other way
beyond the Moor of Rannoch
across the Highlands towards
          Arisaig, Mallaig –
I'm shocked again, this time
by the absence of buildings,
the absence of people. The harsh result
history books only hint at, mythologize.
Brown rolling hills,
beautiful lonely places threaded together
                              with water,
sudden patches of sad dust
no animal will touch.
Didn't someone once live here
and here?

The dried up pod of history rattles
useless seeds. Nights I dream
of someone's bitter lips,
I dream of trying
to understand, of trying to forgive –
of *someone* always wanting to forgive
someone else...
Stories my brain reels out –
from where?

Meanwhile the train takes us farther up,
through rain that seeps in my chest,
rain that eats through tendons, ligaments...
It takes the two of us
and some whisky by a fire
to fight off the icy wet
                    cuts in my feet.

A boat takes us farther
            beyond the Isle of Skye
to the edge of the world I know –
And in the end it's the sky
full of June light until 11:00 p.m.,
a summer sky that never gets darker
                            than midnight blue
with a luminous blueberry sheen
revives me, keeps me watching
for something more.

Love in a Bathtub

Years later we'll remember the bathtub,
the position
            of the taps
the water, slippery
as if a bucketful
            of eels had joined us...
we'll be old, our children grown up
but we'll remember the water
                    sloshing out
the useless soap,
the mountain of wet towels.
'Remember the bathtub in Belfast?'
we'll prod each other –

Belfast, November 1987

You are the perfect journalist:
Clear-eyed. Never at a loss
for balanced words.
I am the one who gets lost,
who still lingers over the smell of burning turf
from yesterday's visit to the museum.

And that is how we walked in
to the pub on Falls Road:
talking about turf fires
and the old way of thatching roofs
and the new way of building playgrounds.
How does one begin
to understand a place, a time?

2

She said her name is Maggie.
She said she's sixty-five-years-old.
Perhaps she started
talking with me because
I was the only other woman in the pub.
It was almost empty that night.

Old banged-up wooden doors
                  hang crooked.
We take our beers to the back room.
Thick turf-smoke
fights the permanent smell of cigarettes.
But we are well-protected
from the November gales outside.

Was I interviewing her
or were we simply two women talking?

All the techniques I learnt from you,
all the notes I took
    I kept to myself.

She said her name is Maggie.
And she sat in her chair
as if she always chose this corner.
Her fingers were cold bones.

Her eyes, grey
shot with a wild blue.
And such a sad cunning in her smile.
We sat talking for three hours, maybe four –
about the usual things: families.
Brothers, sisters . . . Her sons.
The wars she survived.

And even an ungrateful niece
visiting from Australia, who didn't want
the strident white fake diamond earrings
Maggie finally made me wear
just so she could see how the flash
against black hair
        even if they are fake –

'You keep them, luv,'
      she said –

'You keep them.'

29 April 1989

She's three-months-old now,
asleep at last for the afternoon.
I've got some time to myself again
but I don't know what to do.
Outside everything is greyish green and soggy
with endless Bremen-Spring drizzle.
I make a large pot of Assam tea
and search through the books
in my room, shift through my papers.
I'm not looking for anything, really,
just touching favourite books.
I don't even know what I'm thinking,
but there's a rich round fullness
in the air
like living inside Beethoven's piano
on a day when he was
particularly energetic.

The Need to Recall the Journey

for Regina Munzel

Now when she cries
    for milk,

now as she drinks
    I drift back
to the moments when she was
almost out

still part of me
but already I could reach down
      and touch her hair.

I want to return
to her moment of birth.
It was too quick.
I want it to go on –

When the pain was suddenly
defined by her head,
when she was about to slide out
      safely
all by herself – I felt my heart
go half-way out with her...
like seeing a beloved one off
to a harbour, to a ship
destined to go
to a far away place
      you've never been to...

But I could touch
      her hair –
a thick, fuzzy heat.
Sticky feathers clung
wet to runny whites of eggs...

But this is a little person
who already has
a favourite sleeping position.

Weeks pass, the bleeding stops.
Months pass –
What I thought could never heal
actually heals.

And still there is this need
to recall the journey,
retell the story.
The urge
to reopen every detail
until our faces glow again.

What are we
trying to understand?

How we walked for hours
while *she* kneaded herself
out of my womb;
how we paced up and down
the small room – circling
the huge bed.

No one can explain these details.
No one could have prepared
         me for this.

The sound of ripping
silk, tearing skin
comes from within me.

Machines are recording everything
one might like to know.

Afterwards, I thought:
how lucky to have been alert
as any animal
struggling to give birth

in a cave

or behind a grove of trees

or in an open field

now walking, now straining to push,
now lying down
without drugs – no anaesthesia.
How lucky to have felt
each step. The sharp
scalping blackness
as if one had swallowed
thorns, entire cacti
and splinters from a knife...

Fallen fruits burst
into slippery juice.

Fat roots that once pulled
sucking up salt:
sobbing voices from the sea –
fat roots let go
          snap away
then break apart like rubber pipes
full of blood.

Is this how it feels
to be almost drowned?

          Black, black,
          that old knowledge
          from the earth.

And I stopped
listening to T-Bone Walker
and then Telemann, I was told
spinning out loud from the cassette.

How everything irritated
me except your hands
        your voice.

No one can explain
        these details.

A thousand rivers collided
        rushing
and changed direction
within my chest.

And then, she was out
she was taken away
to be washed, bathed –
She was taken to be examined.

And then, I was cold.
Cold, as if my bones
had been emptied
        of their marrow.

At the Flower Market

When we go to the flower market,
my daughter and I,
it's only to look around
not to buy.
For me it's to look at her
six-month-old face while she stares
at the colours and smells
the sour oozing of cut stems
the sweet soil of potted plants.
So many different leaves thrown together,
petals ruffled and fanning out so
even the least fragrant flowers *are* fragrant.
The lilies fighting giant sunflowers
for attention; rows of herbs arranged
beside tall *ficus benjamins*.

Today I stop by the expensive hibiscus
and bougainvillea, imprisoned
in plastic pots they sit like laboratory specimens
because this is Bremen.

In Poona
our bougainvillea bush
had grown to the size of an elephant.
The mauve bracts surrounding the flowers
would fly in the wind
like a thousand miniature paper kites.
And the hibiscus, so abundant,
those red trumpets with tongues
like golden worms curling out.

Still, I go by every stall in Bremen's
city centre flower market –
for no reason
except to watch my daughter's face open,
her confused curiosity
that makes me plan journeys.

Sinking into the Solstice

December fourth or fifth,
sinking into the solstice,
I'm finally beginning to enjoy
the darkness, even the Bremen blackness,
damp and rotting, and conquered
by crows whose late afternoon cries
are not hollow but fermenting with persistent ghosts.
Oh they are huge mosquitoes as they clamour,
swarming over the Bürgerpark.
When I hear them I think of everything at once:
stale chapatis tossed out to whoever can get them;
pomegranates, Demeter, pine cones,
graveyards, Shakespeare, ten inches of snow,
foghorns, lighthouses, Ted Hughes,
not to mention Edgar Allan Poe and Bombay...

It is December fourth or fifth,
about six thirty in the morning
when I sit up thinking someone
is shining a searchlight on us
or could it be a new street lamp
just put up yesterday outside our window?
No, no, it's only the moon
I end up staring at, only the plump, full
moon filling up our window.
He, she, it, hermaphrodite moon,
changing its resilient sex
as it crosses over borders
from one country into another,
accommodating every language, every idea –
this chameleon moon
is laughing with white fish stuck in its
triumphant white teeth.
Only the moon laughing at me
who still wants it dark,
who still wants to sleep.

Until Our Bones Prevent Us from Going Further
for Michael

We spent all day
        in a jeep –
our hands awkward
with questions, our speech twisted
with confusion as the jeep strained
winding higher and higher through the mountain,
                at eye-level with flying eagles –
we stared back at a vulture who possessed
                  the only tree for miles…

Now the sky begins to feel
like a ceiling we can just barely touch,
maybe
by springing up and then uncoiling
stretching out with a snap
           until our bones
prevent us from going further.

The sky is taut wet silk:
        someone's blue wings,
               panting through a sweaty gleam –
      someone's blue kite
           longing to melt.

It is the sort of blue that makes us
think we can find
answers to all our questions.
Where shall we live? What shall we do?
Shall we ever
        have a child?

I brought you *here* to unwrap my fears,
to pull out words only the Himalayas
could translate
and rephrase with their ringing echoes.
But now
it is the blue that hisses back
                    silencing us.
Now the red tongue of the sun
licks us until we forget our patterns
our different plots
we thought so important.

We have just arrived
at a *gompa*. But we hide
behind the stones by the entrance, not wanting
to interrupt the flow
of *om mani padma om*
                that ripples through the rows
of boys reciting lessons
                with old monks.

Oxygen-weak air
rushes through our lungs
making our blood dizzy – we shudder
as if someone, some spirit
        who lives in such thin air
were reshaping our brains, our dreams.

We watch as if we too were praying
as if they were praying for us.
There are only stones where we stand.
But something stirs, I feel
        a sliding movement –
What *is* that? Rocks skitter.
My soul skuttling away.

We watch, not daring to move.
Those fresh-blood-maroon robes
ruffled by the wind are the only lotuses,
the only flowers between
the dusty stones and the blue-lidded sun.
The eight-year-old boys
just losing their milk teeth
chant as if they had learnt this rhythm
from some ancient insects
with enormous wings, no longer possible today.
Now they pause, now they follow
the old monks, descending slowly
into a new chant. We are allowed
                    to enter.

And now it is your turn
                to weep, the gold
blue-shadowed dust stings your face
as you turn with the wind, towards
the light, towards the broad chest
of the mountain – you weep
alone, you stand tall
your head thrown back, you weep
and I am still far away
    down at the bottom
looking up, just starting to climb the steps
while you weep because
it is more than beauty, more than truth,
more than suffering, more than the firm gentleness
of this infinite treeless blue that glows
over these maroon robed children –
you weep and weep
and I suddenly know
        never again
will I need to justify
my soul to you.

What Does One Write When the World Starts to Disappear?

for Eleanor and Bob

If only the earth
would rise up
          and turn itself
into a woman –
the way she did long ago
in Vedic times
at the foothills of the Himalayas.
It would be so easy.
There
she would stand
complaining to Shiva:
'My head's been hurting all day –'
                    she would groan,
'and my stomach burns
with all their swords and guns
their missiles, satellites, microphones, radios...
I can't go on like this.
It's about time you did something.'
Then Shiva would frown, this time
there's a seven-headed cobra in his hair.
It rears up, all seven hoods flared –
a huge, angry claw.
Shiva would frown
and the seven-headed cobra
hisses in the right direction
paralysing all the armies
into a definite peace.
It would be so easy.

What does one do
when the world starts to disappear?
Where does one go?
What does one take along?

And who will read our books
tomorrow? Who will listen
to our music, tune the sitars
      and the violins?
I mean, what species?

I too, have a recurring dream
of the morning after.
I see the earth strewn
with gas masks and plastic –
      body bags
  bones rattling
        in the wind.
Perhaps a few lizards
have managed to survive,
a few snakes...
I see them crawling out
      from the rocks
that sheltered them.
I dream
a lizard tail's
rippling dance
through the eye-hole
      of a gas mask.
A snake's forked tongue
flicks out, flicks in,
flicks out again, investigating
the nature of plastic.

Sujata Bhatt was born in 1956 in Ahmedabad, India and raised in Poona. She was educated in the United States, including two years at the renowned Writers' Workshop at the University of Iowa. She now lives in Bremen with her husband, the German writer Michael Augustin, and their daughter. Sujata Bhatt works as a freelance writer and has translated Gujarati poetry into English for the *Penguin Anthology of Contemporary Indian Women Poets*. Her poems have appeared in various British, Irish and American journals. She received a Cholmondeley Award in 1991. Her previous Carcanet book, *Brunizem*, won the Alice Hunt Bartlett Prize and the Commonwealth Poetry Prize (Asia).